DIVINE TALK

Conversation with Holy Spirit

AIVAN SUNDAY

Contents

Chapter	Page
Holy Spirit	6
Tell Him Sweet Words	11
Revelation of Himself	13
Solomon Insight	17
Activating Your Angels	22
Ministering With Angels	27
Angelic CD	35
Housing Angels	35
Gifting	36
Enoch	40
You Don't Worship Angels	42
Angels Appearing Earthly	43
Prayer Power	43
God's Thoughts	47

All publishing rights belong exclusively to King Jesus UK.

Divine Talk

Copyright © 2017 King Jesus UK.

All rights reserved under the international copyright law. No part of this book may be reproduced or transmitted in any form or by any means, electronic or mechanical, including photocopying, recording or any information storage or retrieval system without permission from the copyright holder.

For further information, permission, orders, or comments, contact:

> King Jesus UK
> 83 Ducie Street Manchester
> England, M1 2JQ
> United Kingdom

Emai: contact@prophetaivan.org
Website: www.prophetaivan.org

All scriptures are quoted from the King James Version of the Bible, Authorized King James With Apocrypha Bible And The Book Of Enoch, except otherwise stated.

Chapter 1

Holy Spirit

COME NOW let us reason together says the Lord, what an invitation and a pleasure of heart to know that the creator of the universe delights in a conversation with you.

Oh! how I hope all His people would hearken unto this. Who is wiser and more engaging in knowledge and counsel but the Lord Himself. The wisest of men and great of minds in different generations sought counsel from all depths of life, but how pleasurable is them who receives instructions from the Spirit of God. The Spirit that forms all things and created them for His own pleasure and yours too. I esteemed His words more than my necessary food said Job. The great King David said divine conversations has made him wiser than all his enemies.

Divine conversations birth the greatest pleasure on earth, **talking with the maker removes the fear of men. He who talk divine talk dominion and dominion is to him who responds to divine thoughts**. Words are powerful they establishes one reign on earth.

Oh! what's an access to talk divine, the Holy Spirit welcomes its an enjoys it, He establishes all His pleasures by it and gave us access to His thoughts. The holy Scripture is a book of divine conversations, He love it so much he referred to Himself as His conversations, (the word).

Conversation the most precious skills in life, the greatest of minds has learned and master the arts of communication. **Learning to talk to Him bring favor with Him, those who learned to talk with Him become the masters of life**.

If you talk with Him you become skilled in talking with men. Trivializing His thoughts have made many the talk of shame. And I believe you reading this book are in the first equation. Out of heaven He made you to hear His voice! are you hearing His voice? I ask! Many have pursue diverse pleasure on the earth but never received to themselves fulfilment of the desire they pursue, Oh! how can one desire real pleasure and find it when pleasuring their making is very far from their thought? I have always know and had great understand of this, that my pleasure is derived from pleasuring Him.

I am a jealous God saith He, this is a light, a map to life to the wise, a refuser to pleasure Him have usually resulted in diverse experiences of grieve! Ask those who have been known to rebel.

Developing a conversational skill with Him is necessary for those who desire His thought. Those who are graced with depth in the revelation and library of heaven are a people who talk to Him constantly, examine such a one and you will testify of their profound thoughts. A thought of man is never a thought from God, an inspiration from a wise one is merely acceptable from heaven, a wise man never means one who is learned and read volumes of books, but rather he who receive divine thoughts and inspiration from above! This is consider wise in His sight. Oh! brethren if we seek for divine instructions as we do daily for gains and desire His voice as for meat, then His thoughts will becomes our thoughts and His mind as some who have the mind of Christ. Then will the work of His hand retain dominion again and the creation will see the manifestation of the sons and daughters of God.

Accessing His voice is a decision just like any other devotion one may make in their lives, through needs and desire decisions are taking daily to impact change and alter the directions of life. A man woke up, set his goals, in five years I am going to marry a beautiful maid who gives me and delights in my pleasure he said! What a great goal, four years down the line a dream comes through. A dream accomplished makes any man glad and births motivation for greater goal. A business woman say our sale target in six months is to increase two percent, in four and half month target is reached. And the mind is refreshed.

These are decisions that brought about great change, and increase the happiness of the mind, we make decisions daily that instantly or timely affects our focus and productivity for success, these have been the traits of men. Oh! likewise my friends such decision to embrace His presence will profit exceedingly. His love and friendship can be assimilated into our daily walk, doing this will establish once fruitfulness and operations on the earth and secure everlasting righteousness. It is a decision friends, a decision. If you be willing and Obedient, you shall eat the good of the land. (Isaiah 1:19 reads).

He is waiting for you to welcome Him into your affairs, receive Him into you life and begin a joyful walk. He is the Spirit of joy. The laughter of men and the warmest of hearts gives us comfort, **but joy is a spirit that visit and comes from the Holy Spirit**, men become sorrowful when they lack the oil of gladness and the Spirit of God makes one glad, friends establish a relationship with Him that He may reveal to you your inheritance in Christ and bring you to your wealthy place. Your walk with God without Him cannot be complete, many are frustrated in the kingdom because They left Him alone, you cannot leave Him alone and walk with Christ.

You need Him and He is here present to help you. Whom you love you invest time, the prove of love is the investment of time, **you cannot love Him and not be loved by His treasures and all the treasures of the earth are His**.

I love them that love me; and those that seek me early shall find me. Riches and honour are with me; yea, durable riches and righteousness. My fruit is better than gold, yea, than fine gold; and my revenue than choice silver. I lead in the way of righteousness, in the midst of the paths of judgment: **That I may cause those that love me to Inherit substance; and I will fill their treasures**. (Proverbs 8:17-21).

You may say! how do I start and begin a relationship with Him. Receiving Jesus is the greatest gift to us all, believing Christ from your heart is your access to His Holy Spirit, obedience to His teachings give you favour and wisdom in the sight of God. I pray in the name of Christ, before you finish reading this book you will experience divinity.

Say this prayer with me Lord Jesus, come into my heart, wash me with your precious blood and save my soul today, I receive your Holy Spirit to Help me serve you, I thank you merciful Father for my salvation, and I celebrate your glory! Glory.

Separate yourself from sin and invite Him, He is holy and requires a heart crying for change, and a renewing mind for correction and instruction is His delight, sanctify a place and meet with Him DAILY, sing to Him, He love singing. A chapter a day on these three wisdom books will profit you greatly:

Daniel, Job, Proverbs. He that work with the wise become wise, walking with these wise men will impart you greatly.

Any future that lacks preparation will end up in frustration, so make up your mind for greatness, it a decision my precious friend, a decision.

This book will show you how to develop your conversations with Him. Learning and engaging in divine conversation will provoke and birth divine thoughts, the greatest minds are a people of thoughts, thoughts provokes imaginations, imaginations produces visions, vision birth greatness. I will say this again! **the greatest minds are a people of thoughts, thoughts provokes imaginations, imaginations produces visions, vision birth greatness**.

Who is he of a great estate and more qualified to seat under his feet than the Holy Spirit of wisdom. King Solomon new this and received an inheritance Of greatness.

In his book the wisdom of Solomon the wise king revealed his insights to wisdom. Oh! let's that depth and insight be accessible for me, Oh! that all Christian and sinners alike would know this and apply their minds and understanding to know Him. then would they begin their walk towards a glorious palace.

Chapter 2

Tell Him Sweet Words

Oh! mighty Holy Spirit when I converse with you, you listen, you gloriously voice back to me with your thoughts and I take heed and exteemed your wisdom. Holy Spirit the power of the Lord. your profound thoughts have set me in great estate, your knowledge had established my dominion and might over my enemies and foes.

I am a joyful student of your personality, mind, presence and knowledge, your teachings includes mastering and creating joy. I delights in coming to you daily for counsel, and your instructions are my desire, they are cherished more than many precious gold.

I have mastered focus through your thoughts of discipline, in them are the joy and pleasure of my life. I celebrate my sweet fellowship with you. Your manifested presence around me and in my secret place gives me inspiration and great calmness. Oh! that your people will know you. Marvelous Holy Spirit, I ask you reveal your sweet self to your People. A people, the work of your hand. Your breath is in them. Oh! we welcome you, come and take your rightful place in our temple, you are the owner of it. My precious teacher, your manifold inspirations gives me access to the word of truth.

But as it is written, Eye hath not seen, nor ear heard, neither have entered into the heart of man, the things which God hath prepared for them that love Him. **But God hath revealed them unto us by His Spirit: for the Spirit searcheth all things, yea, the deep things of God.** For what man knoweth the things of a man, save the spirit of man which is in Him? **even so the things of God knoweth no man, but the Spirit of God.** (1 Corinthians 2.9-11).

You are the revealer of God's secret, you know the thoughts of the Father. I ask in the name of Jesus you reveal and make know to me those precious things that are freely mine. Help me access the Father's blessing and daily bread due me this day. Make known unto me my provisions reserved before the foundation of the earth. Oh! Wonderful Spirit of God, you are my master mentor I am your delighted student, I enjoys your company, your words of comfort and inspiration are too wonderful for me. Acceptable words aren't enough and never can comprehend my appreciation and honor toward the manifold love, grace and pleasure you continuously showered toward me.

In the sights of flesh I was not qualified neither was I found good in the arena of men. Accusations on the mouth of the simple and their judgments are before me daily. And these rebellious angels casted down, who became demons and the evil spirits they birthed on the earth has made me their focus for destruction, but I found "Teshuva" in your sight your unmerited grace and favour. Your eyes are never that of men neither is your judgment and decision to pleasure the unjust.

Chapter 3

Revelation Of Himself

Oh! that's memorable and unforgettable morning! January 9, 2014. 9 o'clock thereabout you revealed yourself to me in a vision upon my bed. Oh! He walked in, in majesty and decked Himself in glory, His majestic excellent and countenance altered my visage, I was exusted and taken in an awe. Oh! what a joyful day the greatest morning of my life, He came majestically and departed gloriously, leaving me with an angelic and heavenly song to minister with my ministering angels and hosts, to enter His presence and welcome Him thereafter. My precious friends He loves singing, sing love songs to Him.

"Holy Spirit the power of the Lord thou art welcome when thou come home. Holy Spirit the power of the Lord thou art welcome when thou come home".

AIVAN SUNDAY

Oh! what an encounter the revelation on that day altered my life. Precious family hearken to this, you are one dream away to see Him! He is a person. Our Lord Christ my coming King lived amongst men a person on His earthly missions. Oh! the Holy Spirit is a person waiting for your invitation to reveal in you Christ, the Father and His glorious kingdom. What A helper! departs from sin He is holy, renew your mind and think like Christ, He is a Spirit sing to Him spiritual Hymns, the Father has sent Him to your help. Oh! gracious Holy Spirit it is not by mine power neither is it mine might or wisdom it is You, Spirit of God.

My greatest ideas are a reaction from your whispers, my wisdom comes from your thoughts, my joy and focus is rooted in your presence, I birth my inspirations by bowing my ears to your instructions, I saw my hope and future in you then I became a dancer and celebrator of life, reasoning with you all day long has enlarged my mind than the learned. Understanding your counsel had puts me in a great estate and increased my productivity than many in my lineage. Oh! Holy Spirit you are wisdom, I celebrate you profoundly for you are my understanding. Many labour daily for your experience but your presence are ever with me.

Make me Holy Spirit your greatest protégé, your choice student and learner, **I am delighted in receiving your instructions for they carry with them great profits and pleasurable rewards**. And may who rebel against your instructions are near folly, poverty, and shame

I enjoy you Spirit of the living God, **my highest goal is to be your greatest host and pleasure on the earth**.

Teach me how to pleasure you, show me how to please you, inform me of your delights, that which you derive your pleasure, make me know your grieves and I will abhor them. Your inspirations birth the holy Scriptures, therein you communicated with your people. I am very attentive to your voice. I rebel against any thoughts of trivializing your words.

I love it when you speak, my entire being is revived when your glorious voice is heard. Your whispers are greatly cherished, that still small voice which I love. **I pays great attention to it, this is my life, keeping me in the paths of peace, revealing good and evil on the streets. I thank you Holy Spirit for making me productive for my precious Christ**.

How can one live a life of pleasure? without pleasuring and becoming a pleasure to his maker. You have created all things for your pleasure those who pleasures you are pleased by your creation.

By your bare naked hand have you formed me, Oh! out of the desire of your heart have you made me. **You have made me for your own pleasure my deepest desire is to pleasure you and be enjoyable in your sight, and be pleasured by you**.

Most gorgeous Holy Spirit you are the revealer of

secrets you know the secrets of men. The deepest of things are never hidden from you, you are aware of all the happenings on the earth. The activities of the rebellious devils and powers are very wide open to your sight. Oh! Oh! Holy Spirit establish me as your scepter and government on the earth. Use me to reflect your attributes and your love. To holpen the feeble hands, to imprint your wisdom unto the simple. A rod that's bring sinners to Christ, let your counsel in my lips be accepted by the unlearned. Let's men cry for your instructions as they would for a maid. **By your instructions I became a profit to my generation and inherit great substance from God**.

Oh! marvelous Jesus I thank you for sending me your Holy Spirit, I celebrate you for giving me a comforter to comfort me and birth hope within me during hours of despair. During your earthly walk you walked closely with Him, never did you spoke ill nor less of Him, nor was He grieved by you, and Christ was called the Son of the Holy Ghost. Oh! that's your people know this and remove from their station the spirits of religion that causes them to error in the knowledge of the holy one.

Receiving Jesus, the ladder of grace took me out of darkness and the ministry of mercy welcomed me to light.

Oh what a glorious beginning with Christ. satan and his rebellious fellows fought against my salvation why should he leave my kingdom he said. he forecast his wicked devices against my life, his co-working demons, whom I now judged, worked craftily in my dreams during the night season. **I knew I needed a helper with great might**, who do I call? I asked, my acquaintances and families alike, likewise needed deliverance themselves. **Then I made wholehearted and sincere prayers with supplications to my God many a time professing how feeble I was**. He heard my cries and sent forth His Holy Spirit, the Spirit of joy. He came in majesty and arrayed himself in glory defeating my enemies and securing my victories.

Now I knew I must keep Him. This clearly was not by my might never was I in the power but the Spirit of God who has became my trusted help. He came and took His rightly positioned in my tabernacle and never left knowing my body was made by Him and for Him alone. He also introduced me to His angel of His presence who carries His personality alike and impact His wisdom toward men. Oh! precious Holy Spirit you've always made yourself known to the students of your wisdom, you come swiftly to him that treasure your instructions and delights in your counsel.

Chapter 4

Solomon Insight

Have you ever wondered how King Solomon received his wisdom and became mighty in deed? We are well told the greatness of his wisdom.

And God gave Solomon wisdom and understanding

exceeding much, and largeness of heart, even as the sand that is on the seashore. And Solomon's wisdom excelled the wisdom of all the children of the east country, and all the wisdom of Egypt. For he was wiser than all men; than Ethan the Ezrahite, and Heman, and Chalcol, and Darda, the sons of Mahol: and his fame was in all nations round about. (1 Kings 4:29-3).

Many had failed to comprehend that wisdom is a person called the Holy Spirit, He is the Spirit of wisdom one of His many missions on earth is to testify of Jesus, and of His kingdom. **He takes the thoughts of the Father and revealed them to mankind and that becomes their wisdom**.

Prophet Isaiah in the eleventh chapter of his writing prophesied the Spirit of wisdom coming upon Christ the Messiah which was confirmed by the baptism by John, this Spirit was on Him without measure because He was the Son of the Holy Spirit. This confirms His saying that greater than Solomon is here.

Yes God had promised the young King Solomon wisdom to lead His people Israel but for that promise to become a testament in Solomon's life the young king would have to engage divine help from God's power.

It is not by might nor by power but by my Spirit saith the Lord. You may say I pray, I fasted and ask Holy Spirit to come into my life but nothing happened. I believe Solomon had that same thoughts **until he came to understanding and realized He must**

invite the Holy Spirit into his life and engage in a DAILY FELLOWSHIP with Him.

Many are failing in their Christian walk and bearing no fruit, because they have neglected the ability of their helper sent from the throne room of heaven to walk and labour with them.

He is the Spirit of truth who teaches you how to pleasure the Father. When you Know Him and begin to learn from and be led by Him you become the sons and daughters of God.

For as many as are led by the Spirit of God, they are the sons of God. (Romans 8:14).

To live as goD on the earth you need Him.

After trying every attempt to gain and manifest the wisdom God had promised him with little success the young Solomon received understanding and said thus:

Wherefore I prayed, and understanding was given me: I called upon God, and the spirit of wisdom came to me. (Wisdom of Solomon 7:7).

After I am come into mine house, I will repose myself with her: for her conversation hath no bitterness; and to live with her hath no sorrow, but mirth and joy. Now when I considered these things in myself, and pondered them in my heart, how that to be allied unto wisdom is immortality; And great pleasure it is to have her friendship; and in the works of her hands are infinite riches;

and in the exercise of conference with her, prudence; and in talking with her, a good report; I went about seeking how to take her to me. For I was a witty child, and had a good spirit. Yea rather, being good, I came into a body undefiled. Nevertheless, when I perceived that I could not otherwise obtain her, Except God gave her me; and that was a point of wisdom also to know whose gift she was; I prayed Unto the Lord, and besought him, and with my whole heart I said. (Wisdom of Solomon 8:16-21).

We see here a practical application and an investment of time in having acquaintance with Him.

I applied mine heart to know, and to search, and to seek out wisdom, and the reason of things, and to know the wickedness of folly, even of foolishness and madness: (Ecclesiastes 7:25).

I applied my heart to know Him and have a personal knowledge of Him, to search by experiences and sensitivity, this involves yielding toward His leading. To seek Him out this requires a diligent obedience toward holiness and the zeal for His will, then He becomes a friend and a lover.

In his tremendous and life-changing book, good morning Holy Spirit. Benny Hinn talked and delve into how he developed a personal relationship with the Him.

The Spirit of God revealed the father and the Son, He was sent here on earth to labour with us in the work of Christ.

Apostle Paul knew this. To do great exploits in his ministry, he needed to establish a daily conversation with the Spirit of wisdom. In his letter to the Corinthians he wrote these words.

The grace of the Lord Jesus Christ, and the love of God, **and the communion of the Holy Ghost**, be with you all. Amen. (2 Corinthians 13:14).

His daily conversations and acquaintance with Him gave the apostle a profound insight and such boldness that he is exclaimed! I thank my God, I speak with tongues more than ye all: (1 Corinthians 14:18).

He became a master in tongues by talking divine language daily. This relationship he had cultivated and his heavenly language gave the apostle great understanding of divine matters and revelations, insight and depth, even Peter was mesmerized by his wisdom. Those who have cultivated a fellowship with Him increases levels of speaking in tongues and diversity of utterances. **As one grows in heavenly language understanding is giving them and their interpretation becomes fruitful.**

Pastor Benny shared how he would come home from school and hurried up to his room where he would talk with and enjoy the warmth and glorious presence of the Holy Spirit, he enjoyed these fellowship and friendship so much he wouldn't even want to leave his room because of the glory of his manifested presence, when he wasn't home his only desire was to be back in his little room with the one whom had revealed the Saviour to him and graced him with comfort. His revelation has caused many people world-over to cultivate a daily walk with the Spirit of wisdom.

This was the same revelation that Solomon had that gave him a name and greatness amongst men.

He will make you of quick understanding says (Isaiah 11:3). **When Solomon craved for this fellowship he came down and open up his mind for quick understanding to know the deep and the depth of God**. This is the reason why the king had a broad and enlarged hearts because he was able to comprehend deep things and understand divine thoughts. **When you know His thoughts you become the talk of your world**.

Chapter 5

Activating Your Angels

Your angels, they come to labour with you in your assignments. They are released and sent from the throne room of God to guard, lead, they are a couriers and dispatchers of divine messages. This angels varies in shapes, sizes and appearances. Their visitations and human acquaintances are mostly determined by once mission and assignments on the earth. The man Daniel had great encounters with his personal angels based on his mandate. To challenge powers, authorities and territorial spirits. And being made a Scepter to stand for the Israelite.

For mine Angel shall go before thee, and bring thee in unto the Amorites, and the Hittites, and the Perizzites, and the Canaanites, the Hivites, and the Jebusites: and I will cut them off. (Exodus 23:23).

His personal awareness and understanding of angelic activities and visitations is to be admired. These angels brought to him regularly the counsel of heaven and informed him of divine matters. **His understanding of spiritual realms and heavily matters made him an outstanding spiritual seer.**

His access in the spirits realm was so great that God compared his wisdom to see in the spirit world like that of satan who had little hindrance accessing that realm.

Behold, thou art wiser than Daniel; there is no secret that they can hide from thee: (Ezekiel 28:3).

Though satan glory was turned to shame he retained access to spiritual spheres. Daniel could not have such insights of this realm except by the guide of the holy angels who operates in those realms. **Everything done in the spirit is done by angelic beings not humans**, the physical man and his mortal being cannot function there, but their spirit man. Growing in understanding and cultivating discernment demands one to be sensitive to angelic atmosphere. **The knowledge of personal angels profits greatly**. When you are visited of them, their name is made known.

AIVAN SUNDAY

And the angel answering said unto him, I am Gabriel, that stand in the presence of God; and am sent to speak unto thee, and to shew thee these glad tidings. (Luke 1:19).

Their visitation is to guide you in divine will and help you develop and understand your gifts. We read in the book of proverbs and in the wisdom of Solomon, and the King would constantly referred to wisdom as her. This is the reason God exteemed the wisdom of Daniel more than that of Solomon.

Solomon was a wise king **but he that is greater in spiritual understanding have power with God**. Thus: one of the reason he departed from God. He confused the angel of "His presence" of the Holy Spirit that carries His gifts and conveys His wisdom to him, to that female monster Leviathan, she appeared to him as an angel of light, thus they seduced him with many strange women and broke his focus.

And this is how God likened his wisdom, different from that of Daniel because Solomon had greater understanding of earthly matters:

And Solomon's wisdom excelled the wisdom of all the children of the east country, and all the wisdom of Egypt. For he was wiser than all men; than Ethan the Ezrahite, and Heman, and Chalcol, and Darda, the sons of Mahol: and his fame was in all nations round about. And he spake three thousand proverbs: and his songs were a thousand and five. And he spake of trees, from the cedar tree that is in Lebanon even unto the hyssop that springeth out of the wall: he spake also of beasts, and of fowl, and of creeping things, and of fishes. (1 Kings 4:30-33).

Daniel a prophet, **a man who had understanding in all visions and dreams**, distinguish amongst many presidents, who was the epitome of excellent, was baptised and graced with angelic visitations who taught him the realms God dwells. In God throne there are million and millions of angels and angelic beings whom ministers to His glory and billions who attend to His decree.

In spiritual realms heavenly activities, manifestations are carried out and done by angels and their host.
Bless ye the LORD, all ye his hosts; ye ministers of His, that do His pleasure. (Psalm 103:21).

The FATHER conceived an birth His thoughts, the SON voiced it and gives it is a sound (the WORD) and the SPIRIT empowers the word.

The ministration of angels then manifests God thoughts and establishes its in all His dominion.

Then the devil leaveth him, and, behold, angels came and ministered unto him. (Matthew 4:11).

Now the realm of God is a kingdom of order an atmosphere of the truest discipline in governance, satan and the rebellious angels where driven and chased out not by God but rather the upmost discipline of governmental order by the spoken word.

satan thoughts was his own destruction because he's thought came from God spoken word.

For thou hast said in thine heart, I will ascend into heaven, I will exalt my throne above the stars of God: I will sit also upon the mount of the congregation, in the sides of the north: I will ascend above the heights of the clouds; I will be like the most High. (Isaiah 14:13-14).

So when he thought to overthrow God, **he invoked the spoken word upon himself and the word brought him to shame**. God uphold all things by the word of His power.

In the highest realm of God operations are done in thoughts. David understood this very well and God responded to his thoughts to build him a temple, the same night he conceived the thoughts. Friends meditate always on God's love and for His kingdom, pondering on those things that are pure , lovely and of the highest reports.

Now it came to pass, as David sat in his house, that David said to Nathan the prophet, Lo, I dwell in an house of cedars, but the ark of the covenant of the Lord remaineth under curtains: Then Nathan said Unto David, Do all that is in thine heart; for God is with thee. And it came to pass the same night, that the word of God came to Nathan, saying, Go and tell David my servant, Thus saith the Lord , Thou shalt not build me an house to dwell in: (1 Chronicles 17:1-4).

Those who constantly meditates on His love are a welcomer and receiver of ministering angels.

And Mary said, My soul doth magnify the Lord, And my spirit hath rejoiced in God my Saviour. (Luke 1:46-47).

Angels are stewards and guards in the spirit world they are entrusted and responsible for the works of His hand. In the earth realm they impact and teaches the secrets of God. The fallen angels came down and began to teach the children of men evil works and how they are done. **Likewise the holy angels visits for divine revelations, impactions, developments and perfection of gifts**.

Chapter 6

Ministering With Angels

Angels are ministry spirit they minister in the throne of God. They administered to the works of His hand. There are divers of angels that ministered in His presence daily, they have access to His presence because they are a worshipers of His Glory. Not just any song that's bring these angels to His presence rather they minister to His glory by talking His language.

When you talk His language you talk directly to Him, once your voice is heard He return His word back to you and this is the truth and revelation that make great.

His word cannot be received with obedient mind and not lift up the fallen or heal the broken.

For he that speaketh in an unknown tongue speaketh not unto men, but unto God: for no man understandeth Him; howbeit in the spirit he speaketh mysteries. (1 Corinthians 14:2).

When one talk in tongues he talks directly to the Father and the voice of God is heard by the ministration of the Holy Spirit. When one sing spiritual songs, hymns and melodies they enters the realms of angelic ministrations.

Ministering in glory to the Father in heavenly tongue daily invites the ministration of angels. Accepting this invitation to stand in on awe with the angels who ministered nonstop for His glory daily birth access and visitation from holy angels. Angels delights when sent on an errand on earth to visit the children of God.

Likewise this is a great understanding to visualize yourself with the Heavenly host singing and worshiping God. this is done by the power of imagination, visualizing yourself standing in an awe with multitude of angels fellowshipping and praising Jehovah. Many a time mankind have used their power of imagination for unprofitable works and folly. But using these gifts to access His throne is greatly encourage by Him.

Imagination of a fellowship with angels as they

worship and minister to the Father is what gets you in His presence. This is done by creating an atmosphere of spiritual hymns, and melodies, singing with angels and the power of your imaginations takes you to His glorious presence.

Once you entered and have mastered this principle your imaginations to enter are no more needed in this arena but you will begin to see yourself as you minister with these angels in His throne. **Angels minister and sings to God, when you minister to God and sing with them you become their friends and they delights in your visitation**.

Speaking to yourselves in psalms and hymns and spiritual songs, singing and making melody in your heart to the Lord. (Ephesians 5:19).

Those who celebrate divine instructions and delights themselves in obedient toward God are a commander of angels, **when you obey Jesus your Angels and heavenly host pleasure in obeying you**. To whom much is given much is required, moving consciously with angels will demands obeying their voice.

From the beginning of time the Father has established His throne and sat therein, NOW you must get this truth, the Father have seated and have never moved neither will He or having the thought to do so, He has set His government and utter His words which sets His charge, His angels hearken to His decree and His thoughts is produced, henceforth He never fight your battle but His angels delight in that duty, neither is He coming down from His seat to give you food or shake hands with you, these are some of the duty of His angels not God. No man see Him and live but he reveals Himself in multitude and divers manner.

You may say God will do it for me, yes you are right! He sends His ministering spirits, your angel, but will never dethrone Himself.

And about the ninth hour Jesus cried with a loud voice, saying, Eli, Eli, lama sabachthani? that is to say, My God, my God, why hast thou forsaken me? (Matthew 27:46).

If the Father did not come down Himself to deliver His begotten Son, the chance Him coming down to you is very slim. Think about this, God rising early, getting ready to an earthly visit, and some Arose amongst the twenty four elders and also with them, the holy angels and the creatures who dwells In His throne! say thus unto Him, God where are you going? He replied! to a young man named osarobo in the village of ukhiri to bring Him some money, food, or anything you may wish right now! for God to bring to you.

My friend frankly speaking! what will His heavenly hosts, think of that, there is a popular saying in many nativity, a king never goes on transfer, well likewise the creator of the whole universe. This duties has been assigned to divers departments of angels and it is your responsibility to make use of them, they where created to minister to you.

Oh! haleluya I grew and develop my knowledge of them, I counsel you to do likewise, they are waiting for your instructions, **obeying the Lord Jesus guarantee there obedience to you, acknowledging they are around you is a start, ministering with them is a must and those lead by them leads in the arena of life**.

Remember! There are sorcerers, occultists and spiritualist who understands this, likewise they have developed there knowledge in moving and ministering with their demons, we are not talking about them here and never are they received or discussed in our thoughts.

Our focus here is the holy angels who have remained loyal and obedient to the Father's kingdom and this are our friends and brethren, there visitations on earth is greatly received. These angels are the carriers of the things You are currently asking and ignorantly murmuring for, and this things are in offices, store houses and positions where this angels are authorized and empowered to dominate and operates, this is there offices and for the purpose thereof they were creation, this is there inheritance.

Praying Gods will is your access, speaking and commanding your angels to bring what you are asking God for is the chief secret to your manifestation.

And the LORD said unto Moses, Wherefore criest thou unto me? speak unto the children of Israel, that they go forward: (Exodus 15:15).

AIVAN SUNDAY

The children of Israel knew not how to minister to there angels, but Moses the man of God knew that! and had a personal revelation of his own assigned angels, **hence the reason your man of God is working the seer anointing by moving with there angels and many religious folks are not**. Now you know, begin your ministration with your angels who keeps you in the way.

If the devil had this simple knowledge I see no reason you shouldn't profit with this. Listen to what satan says to Christ.

And saith unto him, If thou be the Son of God, cast thyself down: for it is written, He shall give His Angels charge concerning thee: and in their Hands they shall bear thee up, lest at any time thou dash thy foot against a stone. (Matthew 4:6).

satan know the many functions of holy angels, they shall bear thee up, he said, he knew they are to guard and bring you to your inheritance in Christ. Your angels are waiting on your words, God's words in you commands there attention swiftly toward your affairs.

A closed mouth and unbelieving heart rarely sees them. Hence the reason Zacharias was made dumb and unable to speak until his son John the baptist was born, chapter one of Luke pictured this, when the priest saw the angel Gabriel appearing to him to deliver divine message, he was troubled and fear fell upon him,

Oh! what a scene, you may say he must have had an encounter with angels, NO! not so, **those that have encounter angels are never frightened by one**, yes he was a priest of God but lacked the knowledge of this revelation, God will reveal and work with you in accordance with your invitation and understanding of Him. Ever wonder why a man who was after God's own heart cried out and exclaimed! God! give me UNDERSTANDING, and I shall live? **revelation and divine depth is proportionate to once dominion**. Early will I seek thee, to see thy power and thy glory, says the patriarch David.

Many have experienced His healing in their health but rarely see Him in there marriage, likewise he who has the mantle for prayer merely receive the light for financial fortune, **we are all ignorant in some part and the cure to this folly is what you know**.

Unlike the priest, here is Manoah's wife, Samson mother, a woman who was not afraid of divine visitation neither was this experience new to her, her reaction was inspiring because she was in control of the matter, with familiar knowledge she calmly interpreted her visitation to her husband. In her words the angels countenance would have scared her but she was familiar with angelic experiences.

And the angel of the LORD appeared unto the woman, and said unto her, Behold now, thou art barren, and bearest not: but thou shalt conceive, and bear a son. Now therefore beware, I pray thee, and drink not wine nor strong drink, and eat not any unclean thing: For, lo, thou shalt conceive, and bear a son; and no razor shall come on his head: for the child shall be a Nazarite unto God from the womb: and he shall begin to deliver Israel out of the hand of the Philistines. Then the woman came and told her husband, saying, A man of God came unto me, and his countenance was like the countenance of an angel of God, very terrible: but I asked him not whence he was, neither told he me his name: (Judges 13:3-6).

And Jesus knew how crucial His angels are to His ministry, and when they came to take Him, He wasn't fighting with them, **that role is for the warring angels** and neither was He afraid but he said,

Thinkest thou that I cannot now pray to my Father, and He shall presently give me more than twelve legions of angels? (Matthew 26:53).

All He needed to say was to invite them to the scene by asking the Father, and command them accordilly.

You may say I have ask the Father, now begin to invite and command them. The fallen angels came down to teach mankind wickedness, likewise the holy angels comes down teaching righteousness.

David a worshiper and praiser of God. **Many of his inspiration and writings were received through angelic visitations. When angels visits they leave you with a song to refresh your heart. Here was the reason he became a great psalmist, because**

he was receiving and learning new song by ministering with angels for divine inspirations.

O sing unto the Lord a new song: sing unto the Lord all the earth. (Psalms 96:1).

Chapter 7

Angelic CD

Now that you are reading this book, and the spirit of obedience is aroused in your mind, I will counsel you to get the CD, ANGELIC MINISTRATIONS, A must to have with this book, get the angelic songs produce only for this book to help you activate and introduce your angels. The songs in this CDs were inspired by the ministration of angels as they worship and minister to the Father, so worshiping with them in this glorious songs as they worship Jesus will translate you swiftly to the throne room of God.

I will sing a new song unto thee, O God: upon a psaltery and an instrument of ten strings will I sing praises unto thee. (Psalms 144:9).

Chapter 8

Housing Angels

Once you are acquainted with your angels. Their name is revealed their purpose of visitation is made known, then your knowledge of their visibility opens up. You can see their physical shape and appearance around you, they usually take a position and stay there, in many cases they guard that location or territory and exercised dominion over its.

for example the angel of protection will normally take position and stand at the door or top of it, to protect you from satanic oppressions and his devices to suffocate you in the night season.

And the Lord appeared in the tabernacle in a pillar of a cloud: and the pillar of cloud stood over the door of the tabernacle. (Deuteronomy 31:15).

Most times these angels are around you without your realization. Just playing these CDs at your homes will open up your eyes to see them in their duties.

Visit our site for CDs, & Books
www.prophetaivan.org

So he drove out the man; and he placed at the east of the garden of Eden Cherubims, and a flaming sword which turned every way, to keep the way of the tree of life. (Genesis 3:24).

And these angels moves with you leading and guarding you. They show you the way you shall go.

Behold, I send an Angel before thee, to keep thee in the way, and to bring thee into the place which I have prepared. (Exodus 23:20).

Chapter 9

Gifting

When you receive Jesus you also receive His Holy Spirit what you do with His Spirit determines how far you go with God. This is what determines your greatness in the kingdom.

Hence is the reason Solomon laboured and developed His intimacy with Him and this was the truth behind apostle Paul exploits and the ministry of our living Christ. As your relationship grows in Him he releases angels to perfect your gifting by this your angelic visitation is sure.

For to one is given by the Spirit the word of wisdom; to another the word of knowledge by the same Spirit; To another faith by the same Spirit; to another the gifts of healing by the same Spirit; To another the working of miracles; to another prophecy; to another discerning of spirits; to Another divers kinds of tongues; to another the interpretation of tongues: But all these worketh that one and the selfsame Spirit, dividing to every man severally as he will. (1 Corinthians 12:8-11).

We see here apostle Paul talking about the nine gifts of the Holy Spirit and they are also called the Spirits of wisdom, knowledge, and so on. In other words they are referred to as spirits but this is difference from the person of the Holy Spirit.

Christ as a person have a personality and office likewise the Father. The Holy Spirit in His office is the one who empowers these nine gifts to function in there ministries and operations. Many have misplaced

His position as the doer and worker of these gifts. I have even heard some called or refer to Him as their messenger **but rather the power and source of their messenger who is the angel**.

And this have robbed many of their angelic visitation by confusing the Holy Spirit who is the Source and Power with the angel the Father has sent to guide and bring them to their heritage. **Angels are your ministering spirit not your Holy Spirit**.

Are they not all ministering spirits, sent forth to minister for them who shall be heirs of salvation? (Hebrews 1:14).

You and I are empowered by the Holy Spirit, the angels derives their strengths and operations from the Spirit of God. The archangel Micheal is a minister of defence, (warring angel) as one of the highest ranked angels, he wages war against outside forces and dominates God's realm. he is an angel functioning as a warrior but he is a spirit, so likewise are the angels of God, the angel of wisdom, discernment, prophecy, prosperity, healing and understanding and so on, these are offices whereby they function and they derive their strength from the Holy Spirit of God.

In (Ephesians 1:17-18) Paul prayed a revelational prayer, that the angel of wisdom that which Solomon was acquainted with and the angel of revelation and knowledge, these are cherubs guarding the knowledge of God, during the fall of Adam they where dispatched to guard the garden and the tree of knowledge, they are seen in the ark of God guarding the testament (ten commandment, the Word, the wisdom and the knowledge of God).

They visit many who spend time in God's word and in obedience toward divine instruction regularly, this angels revealed to them pictures and expand the word of truth as they read and meditate in it.

Then opened He their understanding, that they might understand the scriptures, (Luke 24:45).

In the prophetic ministry the angel for revelation is well known and the angel of wisdom is received by those who labour and establish intimacy with the person of the Holy Spirit and the word.

I love them that love me; and those that seek me early shall find me. (Proverbs 8:17).

God created everything by His wisdom the person of the Holy Spirit.

By His Spirit he hath garnished the heavens; His hand hath formed the crooked serpent. (Job 26:13).

His Spirit was delighted for the works He had made, when your goals and desire are achieved rejoicing follows and the mind is refreshed, a state of ecstasy is observed. Having accomplished this great feet. He decided to visit His precious humans He had created on the earth. He came to His own calling and they received Him not.

Doth not wisdom cry? and understanding put forth

her voice? She standeth in the top of high places, by the way in the places of the paths. She crieth at the gates, at the entry of the city, at the coming in at the doors. Unto you, O men, I call; and my voice is to the sons of man. O ye simple, understand wisdom: and, ye fools, be ye of an understanding heart. (Proverbs 8:1-5).

Likewise the first coming of Christ on the earth to a people He made from the beginning and they reviled, hated and even killed him. But He rose And went back to whence He came likewise the Holy Spirit in His days.

Chapter 10

Enoch Chapter XL11

1, Wisdom found no place where she might dwell; Then a dwelling-place was assigned her in the heavens. 2, Wisdom went forth to make her dwelling among the children of men, and found no dwelling-place: Wisdom returned to her place, and took her seat among the
angels.

The person of the Holy Spirit returned and took His place from whence He came. His personality was grieved, His own creation whom He had formed delighted in folly. Having seen the desires of men He commissioned and embodied an angel to carry His personality and presence (angel of wisdom) and took His rightful seat in the throne room of God. Now the angel of His personality which many have referred to as (her) and many a time come as a female angel was now being sent to represent Him on the earth.

And God said thus concerning His Holy Spirit.

Beware of Him, and obey His voice, provoke Him not; for He will not pardon your transgressions: for my name is in Him. (Exodus 23:21).

And Christ said a sin against Him shall not be forgiven.

Solomon encounter this angel of wisdom who give him much revelation and depth of things, and the king in his conversations referred to (wisdom) this angel as her. The Holy Spirit Himself still manifest and make Himself known to many this day, making Himself known to them not as an angel of wisdom but the Person of wisdom. Angels would normally appear as an angel of resemblance, presence or personality, meaning they may take a face of any human known or unknown to you and utter words conveying a divine message.

Many a times people don't understand this. that they have witness and heard an angel in their dreams and visions.

Then there came again and touched me one like the appearance of a man, and he strengthened me, (Daniel 10:18).

This is the reason you may see someone speaking to you your dreams. What you are seeing is the angel of his personality, resemblance or presence, his personal angel taking his face to convey divine message. In most cases these men and women have been able to develop their understanding and personal knowledge of their angels whereby God uses their faces to releases His instructions. This angels may choose not to reveal their appearances and glory for you not to worship them.

Chapter 11

You Don't Worship Angels

Angels are God watchers sent to minister and guard your paths. They are here to guide, guard, and show you heavenly realms. Holy angels are not to be worshiped and nether demand or accept any worship from anyone. They delights in the works of God and hearken unto His voice to visit His people on earth, to labour in the work of Christ. They arrayed themselves in beauty and carries the awesomeness of God's glory. John the revelator with all his understanding and visions falls down to worship an angel who had visited him.

And I John saw these things, and heard them. And when I had heard and seen, I fell down to worship before the feet of the angel which shewed me these things. Then saith he unto me, See thou do it not: for I am thy fellowservant, and of thy brethren the prophets, and of them which keep the sayings of this book: worship God. (Revelation 22:8-9).

Chapter 12

Angels Appearing Earthly

When these angels are sent from the throne room of heaven to dwell with them in charge of God's mandate on the earth, they may take any form other than their original being, but the human mind cannot comprehend their magnificent form when they appear physically in their glory. Hence they are known to take the form of creatures and birds are associated with them. Taking these forms they make themselves known to these individuals. Discernment and divine communications are established and these can be sent for an errand.

And it came to pass at the end of forty days, that Noah opened the window of the ark which he had made: And he sent forth a raven, which went forth to and fro, until the waters were dried up from off the earth. Also he sent forth a dove from him, to see if the waters were abated from off the face of the ground; (Genesis 8:6-8).

We saw in the garden of Eden satan an angel of darkness taking the form of a serpent to deceive Eve and the falling angels taking shapes and forms of all manners of creatures, so likewise the holy angels may take their abode and dwell as they choose.

Chapter 13

Prayer Power

Their appearances and countenance is known by a

person of prayer. Spirit led prayer is one of the secrets in activating your angels when one is endowed with grace to pray and understands heavens reaction it. One is guaranteed an angelic visitation, **when one masters praying God's will, angels are released coming down to establish those requests on the earth**.

He saw in a vision evidently about the ninth hour of the day an angel of God coming in to him, and saying unto him, Cornelius. And when he looked on him, he was afraid, and said, What is it, Lord? And he said unto him, Thy prayers and thine alms are come up for a memorial before God. (Acts 10:3-4).

As a believer of Christ you are giving the authority over the earth, not angels! you, yes you! But mankind has lost his dominion and handed fallen angels their territory. Now there are demons over certain areas operating as a prince in these domain and some of those demons has been operating for thousands of years, taking back your territory and uprooting these forces, **you need power! And this come by fasting and prayer and the help of your angels**.

See, I have this day set thee over the nations and over the kingdoms, to root out, and to pull down, and to destroy, and to throw down, to build, and to plant. (Jeremiah 1:10).

Daniel knew this, an open truth for those living in reality! the operating demons in Daniel territory had became a chief. In fact the tenth chapter of Daniel referred to them as prince, and the mission Of Daniel was set, **he had to be violent in spirit realm because only the violence take their inheritance by force**. Daniel had to become a prayer himself to release his personal angels as they were being delayed on their journey. If your destiny is great there are strong forces in the spirit realm that will try to withstood and hinder your angels coming to you. **Your prayers releases and empowers your angels to visit you freely on this earth realm**.

You have the authority on this earth. And you authorized their coming by prayer. On their way to you they journeyed the spirit world, in this spheres powers and rulers of darkness tries to hinder their entrance. So your personal angels require your prayers and supplications.

People of prayers are a people of visions, visions carries an angelic visitations, visitations conveys divine instructions, divine instructions obeyed confirms greatness.

You schedule your visitations by empowering your angels through prayers. Impartation and praying in the spirit is what bring them swiftly, when you talk in tongues you talk the father language, when you talk the fathers language, you talk angels. This heavenly language commands angelic attention, and the host of heaven will hearken to your words.

Bless the LORD, ye his angels, that excel in strength, that do his commandments, hearkening unto the voice of his word. (Psalm 103:20).

When the Spirit give you utterance you talk God, one who talks God has become a goD on the earth, and where the word of a king is there is power.

God is entrusting you as His voice on the earth, and when you releases His word He places in your mouth you move and touch the angelic realm. This is the mystery in the realm of prophecy, and is well known by them that labour therein, when the angels are waiting on your words, now at this time whatever comes from your mouth, right there the angels are dispatched to bring forth to manifestation.

This words are utterances giving by the Holy Spirit, this is the utterance the book of acts chapter two talked about.

And they were all filled with the Holy Ghost, and began to speak with other tongues, as the Spirit gave them utterance. (Acts 2:4).

You can build up your language by praying in it daily and constantly as you engage in your daily activities. **This is the realm of power**. Ever wonder why you cant pray more than one hour? Your are limited when you pray with your understanding and satan do sense them.

But when you talk in the spirit you are talking God, satan and his rebellious friends are very deaf to This. This is the wisdom of God, a key to spiritual understanding and empowerment.

Jesus knew this and was mighty in it, (Luke 6:12). say he **prayed and continued all night in prayer to God**, I believe you hears it often people of power praying many hours during the night season and you can't? Why is that? Here's the secret, develop your prayer language daily and this empowers you for your assignment, in this zone **you Hear God daily concerning your walk on the earth**.

But while men **slept**, his enemy came and sowed tares among the wheat, and went his way. (Mathew 13:25). This is the realm of power, challenging satan and his folks is a must here, nobody have authority without dominating this arena, here is the reason Christ prayed all night and God would say to Moses:

And the LORD said unto Moses, **Rise up early in the morning, and stand before Pharaoh**, and say unto him, Thus saith the LORD God of the Hebrews, Let my people go, that they may serve me. (Exodus 9:13)

To conform and maintain your dominion on the earth you must stand before any pharaoh in your life. By the power of Christ I curse and judge any devils fighting you.

Chapter 14

God's Thought

AIVAN SUNDAY

A man after God's own heart, Oh! what a testament! Ever wonder how and why king David found favour with God and was mighty in the thoughts of the creator of the universe, this insight was shared with me as I eat and meditate on the word one evening a while back. Many have acquainted themselves with the word but only few knew His thoughts, the word Himself is a product of His thoughts,

He conceived it in His being before seeing the outcome in His imaginations, right there the Word was spoken and became Flesh.

Few ever know His mind and many has refer to this as the spirit of faith. The truth is this! This is the Spirit of understanding, **Understanding what God does next is the mother of all wisdom.**

The righteousness of thy testimonies is everlasting: GIVE ME UNDERSTANDING, and I shall live. (Psalm 119:144).

Once pain or pleasure is proportionate to once knowledge, what you know is produced from your understanding heart.

Give me understanding according to your word! A man after God's own HEART? here is the interpretation of this prayer, a text that have increased the insight of many.
Give me understanding according to your heart, In other word let me understand your THOUGHTS. Those walking in His thoughts are ahead of the speaking world, they walk in the realm of God, these

are a league of revelators.

In the realm of God everything is done in thoughts and imaginations as discussed in the previous chapters, the earthly realm requires words.

The Pharisee knew the word but Christ was far in thoughts.

They revile their Messiah, they knew a doctrine that God has spoken in time past, He ain't ready to speak Again they assumed, but YOD HEY VOD HEY is a moving and a speaking God, He never cease to utter His voice to those who delight in His counsel.

Let me know your thoughts before you speak it! Said David, Thus! this desire enlisted him amongst the chiefest of men. His prayers was answered and a passage to the school of divine thought was born. And God made know to him secrets known to few.

Let the heaven and earth praise Him, the seas, and every thing that moveth therein (Psalm 69:34)).

Many a church service, praise is limited to mankind, and the worship leader may say! Oh hallelujah may we all rise up to praise and worship God. Oh! glory to His name, we need that greatly but the man David had much depth, he realized and came to understanding that **God was looking for a true worshiper on the earth who will command all His creation to worship Him**.

Since satan was chased out from heaven, have you ever heard an audition in heaven for his replacement? O no the heavens don't want him back, he is a rebellious lad, God is looking for you! Yes you heard it right, the heavens are waiting for you to take and walk in his place, **your consciousness of this will bring you to it. Do you know that God's holy angels are waiting for you to command and lead them into worship**! Oh! How I hope God's people will embrace this. Command them, they are waiting.

satan is commanding many things on the earth to worship and bow to himself, he tried that ERROR with Christ. This here should be your glorious work, commanding angels and their hosts and all the works of His hand.

The three Hebrew children were mighty in this and their testimony is loud in eternity. During their season in the furnace of fire, they prayed a prayer that their forefather David would pray, had they not caught and received this revelation as some of you reading this book now have done, they could have been roasted right there.

Here is a prayer of one who is exercising dominion over all the works of God's hand:

O all yee works of the Lord, blesse ye the Lord: praise and exalt Him above all for ever. O ye heavens, blesse ye the Lord: praise and exalt Him above all for ever. O yee Angels of the Lord, blesse Ye the Lord: praise and exalt Him above all for ever. O all ye waters that be above the heaven, blesse yee the Lord: praise and exalt Him above all for ever. O all yee powers of the Lord, blesse ye the Lord: praise and exalt Him above all for ever. O yee Sun and Moon, blesse ye the Lord: praise and exalt Him Above all for ever. O ye stars of heaven, blesse ye the Lord: praise and exalt Him above all for ever.

O every shower and dew, blesse ye the Lord: praise and exalt Him above all for ever. O all ye winds, blesse yee the Lord: praise and exalt Him above all for ever. O yee fire and heat, blesse ye the Lord: praise and exalt Him above all for ever. O yee Winter and Summer, blesse ye the Lord: praise and exalt Him above all for ever.

O ye dews and storms of snow, blesse ye the Lord: praise and exalt Him above all for ever. O ye nights and days, blesse ye the Lord: praise and exalt Him above all for ever. O ye light and darkness, blesse ye the Lord: praise and exalt Him above all for ever. O yee ice and cold, blesse ye the Lord: praise and exalt him above all for ever. O ye frost and snow, blesse ye the Lord:

Praise and exalt Him above all for ever. O ye lightning and clouds, blesse ye the Lord: praise and exalt Him above all for ever. O let the earth blesse the Lord: praise and exalt Him above all for ever.

O Ye mountains and little hills, blesse ye the Lord: praise and exalt Him above all for ever. O all ye things that grow on the earth, blesse ye the Lord: praise and exalt Him above all for ever. O yee fountains, blesse yee the Lord: praise and exalt Him above all for ever.

O ye seas and rivers, blesse ye the Lord: praise and exalt Him above all for ever. O ye whales and all that move in the waters, blesse ye the Lord: praise and exalt Him above all for ever. O all ye fouls of the air, blesse ye the Lord: praise and exalt Him above all for ever.

O all ye beasts and cattle, blesse ye the Lord: praise and exalt Him above all for ever. O ye spirits and souls of the righteous, blesse ye the Lord, praise and exalt Him above all for ever.

O Ananias, Azarias, and Misael, blesse ye the Lord, praise and exalt Him above all for ever: for He hath delivered us from hell, and saved us from the hand of death, and delivered us out of the midst of the furnace, and burning flame: even out of the midst of the fire hath he delivered us. (The Song of the three children).

Knowing and working in this truth will maximize your functionality in the office of praise, as you grow in this arena holy angels and their host are submitted unto you, they are sent to minister with you and made know to you true worship which the Father seek, when this revelation is embraced you become a leader and an earthly host, hosting the holy angels of God who minister with you in spirit and truth.

In this realm the devil become afraid of you, you are doing on the earth what he had failed to do.

When you begin to function in this realm all His creation will harken to your voice and in return the earth and her elements will voice back to you and your knowledge will increase greatly.

The heavens declare the glory of God; and the firmament sheweth his handywork. Day unto day uttereth speech, and night unto night sheweth knowledge. There is no speech nor language, where their voice is not heard. Their line is gone out through all the earth, and their words to the end of the world. In them hath he set a tabernacle for the sun, (Psalm 19:1-4).

Those who knows His thoughts have left the office of commanding people to praise His name long ago! Now they are commanding His creation to do just that.

Praise ye the LORD. Praise ye the LORD from the heavens: praise him in the heights. Praise ye him, all his angels: praise ye him, all his hosts. Praise ye him, sun and moon: praise him, all ye stars of light. Praise him, ye heavens of heavens, and ye waters that be above the heavens.

Let them praise the name of the LORD: for he commanded, and they were created. He hath also stablished them for ever and ever: he hath made a decree which shall not pass. Praise the LORD from the earth, ye dragons, and all deeps: Fire, and hail; snow, and vapours; stormy wind fulfilling His word: Mountains, and all hills; fruitful trees, and all cedars: Beasts, and all cattle; creeping things, and flying fowl:

Kings of the earth, and all people; princes, and all judges of the earth:

Both young men, and maidens; old men, and children: Let them praise the name of the LORD: for His name alone is excellent; his glory is above the earth and heaven. He also exalteth the horn of his people, the praise of all his saints; even of the children of Israel, a people near unto him. Praise ye the LORD. (Psalm 148).

You are goD's says the Father, so act like Him. Having dominion is not dominating mankind, let them have dominion over the earth saith God, and over all the works of my hand. What a privilege, this saying includes the angels too.

Enoch knew this and applied it. He became a goD and a judge over all fallen angels, they begged him to plead and make supplications to God on their behalf.

Are they pleading with you for tormenting and judging them? Or rather they tormenting you? Oh! I Pray you a vision seating a king and reigning with Christ. Receiving such an image will arouse your goDship on the earth.

Why would satan accuses you? My people are perishing for lack of light, ""revelation He says" insight received by walking with God as Enoch did. This is so, many a perish for lack of light and the entrance of His word has giving many great

light.

How could he accuse you? Being the first failure? And at the time of his folly you wasn't there. When he rebelled against his maker your presence was not felt. By his pride he disrupted the plans of old, if one need accusing who should accuse who?

Enoch was not a babe in this matter and he judge him and all the unbelieving devils.

In my new book, I open up a secret you should know about that lad, shaming him will make you one with God. NEW BOOK. SHAMING satan.

Thine heart was lifted up because of thy beauty, thou hast corrupted thy wisdom by reason of thy brightness: I will cast thee to the ground, **I WILL LAY THEE BEFORE KINGS, THAT THEY MAY BEHOLD THEE.**

God cast him down for you to behold his nakedness and shame, **he is the one with shame not you,** why is he shaming you when his name is shame?

Thou hast defiled thy sanctuaries by the multitude of thine iniquities, by the iniquity of thy traffick; therefore will I bring forth a fire from the midst of thee, it shall devour thee, AND I WILL BRING THEE TO ASHES UPON THE EARTH IN THE SIGHT OF ALL THEM THAT BEHOLD THEE. (Ezekiel 28:17-18).

He defied himself with great iniquities and eternity holds up it records, Oh! precious friend you are redeemed, the blood of Christ has purged you, in the sight of the Father He sees perfection, and He is comfortable with the work He designed.

THEY THAT SEE THEE SHALL NARROWLY LOOK UPON THEE, AND CONSIDER THEE, SAYIN, IS THIS THE MAN THAT MADE THE EARTH TO TREMBLE, THAT DID SHAKE KINGDOMS; THAT MADE THE WORLD AS A WILDERNESS, AND DESTROYED THE CITIES THEROF; THAT OPEND NOT THE HOUSE OF HIS PRISONERS? (Isaiah 14:16-17).

NOW if you are still afraid of satan then I pity you, he is a small man never fear him! I pray you the light of God's word and the spirit of power. he was an anointed cherub a guard and a worship servant, he is not afraid of your book volume neither is he afraid of religious rites, but rather light (revelation in God's word) the things of God are revealed, they are not known but by revelational knowledge.

Hence is the reason you must engage an intimacy with the Holy Spirit of Christ, the revealer of deep and secret things, he take what belongs to Jesus and minister them unto you.

When you delight in His presence He give you some of His gifts, many such gifts made Solomon a talk on the earth, He sends an angel of revelation that carries and bring you information.

DIVINE TALK

AIVAN SUNDAY

....
....
....

Prayer

I pray in the name of Christ, before you finish reading this book you will experience divinity. Say this prayer with me Lord Jesus, come into my heart, wash me with your precious blood and save my soul today, I receive your Holy Spirit to help me serve you, I thank you merciful Father for my salvation, and I celebrate your glory, Glory.

www.ingramcontent.com/pod-product-compliance
Lightning Source LLC
Chambersburg PA
CBHW031429040426
42444CB00006B/750